GEARED FOR GROWTH BIBLE STUDIES

SAINTS IN SERVICE

A STUDY OF TWELVE BIBLE CHARACTERS

BIBLE STUDIES TO IMPACT THE LIVES OF ORDINARY PEOPLE

Written by Nina Drew and Stewart Dinnen

The Word Worldwide

CHRISTIAN FOCUS

CONTENTS

QUESTIONS AND NOTES

ANSWER GUIDE

PREFACE

GEARED FOR GROWTH

'Where there's LIFE there's GROWTH:
Where there's GROWTH there's LIFE.'

WHY GROW a study group?

Because as we study the Bible and share together we can

- learn to combat loneliness, depression, staleness, frustration, and other problems
- get to understand and love each other
- become responsive to the Holy Spirit's dealing and obedient to God's Word

and that's GROWTH.

How do you GROW a study group?

- Just start by asking a friend to join you and then aim at expanding your group.
- Study the set portions daily (they are brief and easy: no catches).
- Meet once a week to discuss what you find.
- Befriend others, both Christians and non Christians, and work away together

see how it GROWS!

WHEN you GROW ...

This will happen at school, at home, at work, at play, in your youth group, your student fellowship, women's meetings, mid-week meetings, churches and communities,

you'll be REACHING THROUGH TEACHING

INTRODUCTORY STUDY

Imagine twelve celebrities seated at a long table. Their names are clearly visible on the table before them as the Master of Ceremonies, microphone in hand, invites comments on the topic of 'Christian Service – Happiness or Hassel?'

MASTER OF CEREMONIES	Ladies and Gentlemen, We're so glad you've been willing to join our panel discussion this evening on the subject 'Christian Service – Happiness or Hassle?' We have invited you because of your background and experience in this area. May I start with you, Mr Mark, and ask whether service was happiness or hassle for you?
MARK	Well, quite frankly, at one stage I really didn't feel it was worth all the hassle. That first trip I made with Paul and Barnabas to Cyprus was a complete flop! Didn't realize the difficulties we'd face in Cyprus and by the time we left for the mainland I'd 'had it' (Acts 13:13).
M.C.	Is that why you left Paul and Barnabas?
MARK	Yes. I couldn't face any more so I went home. But I'm grateful that cousin Barnabas understood and gave me another chance even though Paul refused to have me (Acts 15:36-39).
M.C.	Did Paul ever change his mind about you?
MARK	Well, I'm a modest man. Just read 2 Timothy 4:11.
M.C.	We turn now to Mr and Mrs Eagle (Aquila and Priscilla). You folk seem to have journeyed around the Mediterranean quite a bit. Rome – Corinth – Ephesus – Rome again ... I guess you like travel?
AQUILA	Oh no! Travel in our day was no picnic you know. And we didn't appreciate breaking up our little 'nest' so often – but we did it for the sake of God's work (Acts 18:18, 19).
M.C.	So, was it worth the hassle?

AQUILA and PRISCILLA — Oh, a thousand times! The friends we made – and the tremendous times of worship and fellowship that we had in our various homes – it was terrific. We wouldn't have missed it for anything! (Rom. 16:3-5).

M.C. — We turn now to ask one of the ladies a question. Anna, you seem to have had quite a different form of service. What would you say your joy was?

ANNA — After my husband died, I seemed to be set free to spend much time in prayer. In fact, I found fasting a means of further release from everyday details, so that I could worship the Lord and intercede for others (Luke 2:36, 37).

EPAPHRAS — I'd like to back up Anna here because I believe that intercession was the key to seeing the Colossian believers established in the faith (Col. 4:12).

BARNABAS — May I break in here to confirm the value of fasting and prayer. I was in a meeting once with other Christians at Antioch and it was then that the Holy Spirit revealed God's purpose for Paul and me to move out and travel around telling people about Jesus (Acts 13:14). It was a tremendous experience and I always look back with thankfulness for the clarity of my call.

MARTHA — Of course, there's another side to all this. I'm not undermining the value of this kind of service but the practical things have to be done! I always saw that side as my responsibility but I guess I have to be big enough to see that others are gifted and called in other ways. My sister Mary and I had a few tiffs over this (Luke 10:38-42) and I guess I easily get steamed up when I see so much to be done. I certainly seem to have ended up with that kind of reputation anyway! (John 11:21-24, 39-41).

MARY (The mother of Jesus) — You raised a touchy issue for me when you mentioned 'reputation'. This was my biggest burden in carrying out the unique service that was entrusted to me. I tell you I went through spiritual cartwheels over my unusual pregnancy! It almost broke my relationship with Joseph but of course he's a dear, and being sensitive to the Holy Spirit he saw God's purpose coming through and trusted me. That's how I was able to carry out the task that God assigned to me (Matt. 1:18-20).

PRISCILLA I'm thankful you said that, Mary because this business of trust and understanding between husband and wife is so basic to their successful witness. We went through a lot together in the early days of the church (Rom. 16:4) but the Lord blessed our united witness, unworthy though we were.

TIMOTHY I'm glad you raised the issue of unworthiness. I battled with the issue of a low self-image all through my service. My favourite passage in Paul's letters was that one about God choosing the foolish ... the weak ... the lowly ... the despised ... the things that are not (I Cor. 1:27, 28).

M.C. I believe it was your very limitations that made you so useful, Timothy. All the glory had to go to the Lord! Paul valued you greatly for your selfless sacrificial service (Phil. 2:19-22). Well, this has been a very good discussion. I wonder if I might just pose the question to one or two others who haven't spoken yet ... Stephen, I guess this is a tough question for you to have to comment on – 'Christian Service – happiness or hassle?'

STEPHEN Not really. I know that God prepared me for the end, and of course I was ready when it came. I'm specially pleased that Paul saw it all happening – I'm sure that was the start of the change in his life ... (Acts 7:54-8:1).

PHILIP Stephen, right from the earliest days when we were both elected to care for the widows (Acts 6:1-8) I could see that God's hand was upon you for great things.

STEPHEN I suppose looking after those dear people was a kind of apprenticeship for us.

PHILIP I found caring for them a bigger hassle than moving out of Jerusalem and doing some outreach in Samaria! (Acts 8:4-8).

M.C. What did you find to be your major hassle, Philip?

PHILIP Leaving Samaria just as so many were coming to the Lord and needing to be taught. But from that I learned that none of us is indispensable! (Acts 8:26-30). My happiness was seeing that Ethiopian move off in his chariot praising the Lord for being born again!

ELIZABETH	I think that's an important note you've hit, Philip. Happiness is the by-product of obedience. We certainly found it to be so when God performed a miracle allowing me to carry baby John at a pretty ripe age. It certainly shook Zechariah when the angel told him what was going to happen. I'll never forget his face when he came home from the Temple that night. He was literally dumbfounded! (Luke 1:5-23).
MARY (mother of Jesus)	Remember when I called to see you when you were six months pregnant, Elizabeth? Didn't we have a wonderful praise time, thanking the Lord that we could be His servants in this fantastic way? (Luke 1:35-49).
MARY MAGDALENE	You two certainly hit the high spots but I think I've got more to praise the Lord for. You were two perfectly normal women but Jesus saved me from seven evil spirits which possessed me. You'll never know the peace and release of being set free. That's why serving Him, afterwards, was a 'natural'. What else could I do when He had done so much for me? (Luke 8:2). I think my greatest happiness after that was in obeying His command to go and tell the others, and confirm He really had risen. That really shook Peter! (Matt. 28:1-8).
M.C.	Well there you have it, friends. I think our panel has shown conclusively that – yes – there will be hassles in the service of the Lord, but they pale into insignificance compared to the joy, peace and happiness that are the results of obeying Jesus totally and serving Him wholeheartedly.

DISCUSSION SUGGESTIONS

1. Share a particularly difficult piece of service you performed for the Lord, and describe your reactions afterwards.

2. What hassles do you run into in Christian service? What are the compensations?

3. 'Happiness – a by-product of obedience.' Do you agree with this? Shouldn't happiness be our goal. If not, what should be?

4. Paul says in his letter to the Romans, 'Never be lacking in zeal, but keep your spiritual fervour, serving the Lord.' D. E. Hoste, when asked what was the biggest danger to the Christian servant, said 'Spiritual dryness.' What is the secret of avoiding the latter condition and maintaining the former?

5. What should be our motive in serving the Lord?

STUDY 1

ELIZABETH – PRODUCTIVE IN OLD AGE

QUESTIONS

DAY 1 *Luke 1:5-7.*

a) How is Elizabeth's character described?

b) Can you name any other women in the Bible described as barren, who later gave birth to a baby? (Gen. 11:30; 25:21; 29:31; Judg. 13:2; 1 Sam. 1:2).

c) Do you know of any instances today where God has answered prayer for a child?

DAY 2 *Luke 1:13; 18:3-7; Matthew 7:7-11.*

a) Elizabeth and Zechariah had probably prayed for many years for a child. What lessons can we learn from this?

b) Share any instances you have experienced, or know of, of delayed answered prayer.

DAY 3 a) Elizabeth and Zechariah had the privilege of training their son for the ministry God had prepared for him. How is his character and ministry described in Luke 1:15-17?

b) How can we guide our children so they will become servants of God? (Prov. 22:6; Gen. 18:17-19; Deut. 6:6-7; 2 Tim. 1:5; 3:15).

DAY 4 *Luke 1:25; Deuteronomy 28:4,11; Genesis 17:1, 2; Psalm 127:3-5.*

a) Why was it considered a 'reproach' for a woman to be childless?

b) Rearing children was considered a woman's main means of fulfilment. In what other ways today can a woman find fulfilment? (Titus 2:3-5; Rom. 16:1-6; Prov. 31:10-29).

DAY 5 *Luke 1:39-45; Malachi 3:16.*

a) How did Elizabeth know that Mary was to have a baby?

b) What further revelation did she have about Mary's coming baby?

c) Try to imagine some of the conversation during Mary's three month visit.

DAY 6 a) What effect did the birth of Elizabeth's son have on her neighbours and relatives? (Luke 1:58).

b) If the birth of children is a gift from God, what responsibility does that have on us? (Ps. 127:3; I Sam. 1:11).

c) Unlike Elizabeth we do not expect to have children in old age. What kind of fruitfulness can we pray to have? (John 15:5; Gal. 5:22-23; Ps. 92:14).

DAY 7 *Luke 1:6; 57-80.*

a) What evidence do Elizabeth and Zechariah show of a real oneness reaching through to old age?

b) What further cause of joy did Elizabeth have eight days after the birth of John?

c) Both parents were old at John's birth, so they probably had only a few years to guide him. Yet he became a great man of God. What can we learn from this about the responsibilities of parenthood?

NOTES

As I approached my sixty-fifth birthday with forty years of full-time Christian ministry behind me, imminent changes were upon me. What would the later years of my life hold? Would I stagnate spiritually? God has the answer in Psalm 92:12-15....

> The righteous will flourish like a palm tree,
> They will grow like a cedar of Lebanon;
> Planted in the house of the LORD,
> They will flourish in the courts of God.
> They will still BEAR FRUIT in OLD AGE
> They will stay FRESH and GREEN,
> Proclaiming, 'The LORD is upright.
> He is my Rock,
> There is no wickedness in Him' (M.K.D.)

It is obvious that Elizabeth was a godly woman. She was a descendant of Aaron and married to a priest named Zechariah, a true man of God. Her name means 'God is my oath' and she proved beyond doubt that God never breaks His Word.

Childless Jewish women were looked upon with pity. No doubt Elizabeth felt her barrenness acutely. Maybe the older she got the harder this trial grew for her. She and her husband had prayed long and earnestly for a child, but God seemed deaf to their pleas.

Then the impossible happened. God's prediction came to Zechariah. He couldn't take it in. Elizabeth? A child in her old age? Read the amazing account again in Luke 1:11-25. Can you imagine the scene as the dumb Zechariah seeks to convey the message to Elizabeth? 'God will give you a son who is to be named John.' Elizabeth, too, could have reacted in disbelief but verse 25 seems to indicate immediate and complete acceptance of this answer to prayer:

> 'The Lord has shown His favour and taken away my disgrace...'

For five precious months Elizabeth lived in happy seclusion, contentedly preparing for the birth of her baby. Then she had a surprise visit from her relative, Mary. While they were still greeting each other, and apparently before Mary shared the angel's prediction that she was to be the mother of the Christ-Child, the Spirit of God came upon Elizabeth, the baby leaped in her womb and she declared 'Blessed is she that believed, for there shall be a fulfilment of what has been spoken to her by the Lord.'

One can well visualize the preciousness of the next three months for these two women. The older, spiritually mature Elizabeth, indispensably supportive of her dumb husband, also gave herself to Mary, no doubt seeking to encourage and strengthen her for her return to Nazareth to 'face the music' once news of her pregnancy broke on her family, fiancé and the community. Despite these problems, the two women were full of the joy of the Lord.

When Elizabeth's son was born her 'neighbours and relatives heard that the Lord had shown her great mercy, and they shared her joy' (Luke 1:58). At the circumcision ceremony, when pressure was brought to bear on the parents to name the child after his father, they, true to God's word, declared 'His name is John.' This final obedience resulted in the loosing of Zechariah's tongue and he was free to praise and glorify God.

Life began at 50-60 for Elizabeth, or did it? She had been faithful to and blessed of God all her life, but His greatest blessing came to her in old age. Now she had the task of training up a prophet ... John the Baptist who would prepare the way for the coming of Christ the Messiah.

Points to ponder and pray over ...

1. Where was Zechariah when God's revelation came to him? (Luke 1:9-11)
2. Did Elizabeth live in self-pity or hope? (Luke 1:25)
3. Was Elizabeth sapped of spiritual zeal and ministry while pregnant?
4. What was the predominant ingredient of her spiritual life? (Luke 1:41-45 and 57).

A thought for the young ...

Start NOW to **be** God's person if you want to be effective down the years!

And for the not so young ...

God is the same God, in you and through you, to make you count for Him through all your years.

STUDY 2

MARY – MOTHER IN A MILLION

QUESTIONS

DAY 1 *Luke 1:26-34; Isaiah 7:14.*

a) What do you understand by Mary's question to the angel?

b) God would not fulfil His plan without Mary's consent. What does that teach us about the plans God may have for us?

DAY 2 *Luke 1:39-56; Matthew 1:18-25.*

a) Describe Mary's feelings while Matthew 1:19 was taking place.

b) What would be the effect on Mary of her contact with:
Elizabeth (Luke 1:39-56)?
The shepherds (Luke 2:8-20) and wise men (Matt. 2:10, 11)?
Simeon and Anna (Luke 2:22-38)?

DAY 3 *Matthew 1:20, 21; Luke 1:29-31; Matthew 2:13-15; 19-21; Luke 2:48.*

a) Comment on God's dealings with both Joseph and Mary and how they related to each other in their marriage. Can we learn something from this? (Matt. 13:55, 56).

b) They later had four sons, as well as daughters, before Joseph died (some time before Jesus was thirty). How would widowhood affect Mary's relationship with Jesus?

DAY 4 *John 2:1-11.*

a) What was Mary to understand from Jesus' seemingly ungracious reply (v. 4)?

b) Which verse shows her absolute confidence in His ability to cope? (Note: She had never seen Him perform a miracle.)

c) What would result from our having this same trust?

DAY 5 *Mark 3:20, 21; 31-35.*

a) Why did Jesus not want to see His mother and brothers at that time?

b) Can we learn something from this concerning our own family relationships?

DAY 6 *John 19:25-27.*

a) In what way was Simeon's prophecy, 'A sword will pierce through your own soul also' (Luke 2:35) fulfilled?

b) How far did Mary's love for her Son take her, and what consolations came from that?

c) Can you give further examples of how the privilege of serving Christ is accompanied by great joy and also by sacrifice?

DAY 7 *2 Timothy 3:12; James 1:2-4.*

a) Mary had agreed to be 'the handmaid of the Lord' without knowing all that would be involved. After we have committed our lives to Christ what should be our attitude to unexpected sorrows involved in our service for God?

b) What further bonus do you see Mary receiving in Acts 1:14?

c) Use your imagination to describe her meditations at the close of the Day of Pentecost (Acts 2:41).

NOTES

Mary: Millions of women in the Christianized world bear this popular name. In Bible times, as we've noticed before, names had spiritual significance. Mary originally meant 'bitter' or 'sorrowful'. Although she experienced great joy in surrendering to God's purposes, Mary also suffered intense agony and sorrow of heart and spirit.

Royalty: Scripture makes it plain that this humble village lass came of noble stock. The genealogy in Luke 3:23-31 indicates that she was a descendant of David. Matthew 1:1-17 also shows that Joseph was of the Davidic line. These records establish Christ's legal claim to the throne of David – through His foster-father Joseph, as well as His actual descent from David through Mary. (See also – Isa. 11:1; Jer. 23:5; Acts 2:29-30; Rom. 1:3; 2 Tim. 2:8).

Chosen: Every Hebrew female would be aware of the prediction of Isaiah 7:14 and probably much speculation was made as to who this favoured virgin would be. God's favour fell on quiet, unassuming Mary. Was it her knowledge of the scriptures or her trust in the faithful God of Israel, or both, which brought forth such a positive response to the Heavenly Announcement 'You are favoured ... you will conceive ... you will bring forth a son ... JESUS'? We don't know. We only know she bowed to His sovereign will and was blessed. The pathway of blessing for us, too, is in knowing His Word, responding in obedience, to be assured of His Divine purposes and to co-operate with Him positively in the outworking of His will.

Human Reactions: Questions must have tumbled through Mary's mind. How can this be? I am a virgin! How will my parents react? What about my marriage? What will Joseph say or do? Will they stone me to death? This quiet girl held the secret in her heart and no doubt prompted by the angel's declaration about Elizabeth (Luke 1:36) eventually made her way (return journey 250 kms) from Nazareth to the Judean hills to visit her. An older women, Elizabeth was already miraculously pregnant and about to give birth to John the Baptist. Obviously a woman of God, Elizabeth's spirit witnessed immediately with the news Mary brought and they rejoiced together. Mary was further convinced that 'the Holy Thing to be born of her would be called the Son of God' (Luke 1:35). Son of Mary – human; Son of God – Divine. Oh the mystery and wonder of it all!

Submission and its Fruit: Capitulation to Christ and His purposes does result in JOY. Mary spontaneously broke forth into a song of praise and worship. She rejoiced in God her Saviour – marvelled at the divine privilege He was granting His lowly handmaid – acknowledged the continuing faithfulness of the God of Abraham. She could COMPLETELY TRUST GOD to work out all the imponderables. She could leave all her questions with Him.

Faith Rewarded: God knows how to draw circumstances into line with His will when we walk in obedience to Him. Mary wasn't stoned. Joseph believed her testimony. He acted honourably, lovingly and took steps to shield his betrothed from ostracism and worse. Mary now not only had the direct Word of God to herself and the confirmation of that Word through Elizabeth, but also assurance through God's Word to Joseph. 'Do not fear; take Mary as your wife; that which is conceived in her is of the Holy Spirit' (Matt. 1:20 – free translation).

Problems: Walking in the will of God does not guarantee us a problem-free life! Mary (and Joseph) had problems in plenty. Forced to travel 130 kms to Jerusalem for a census just when the baby was due – no suitable accommodation – her precious son born in an animals' shelter (cave) – fleeing to Egypt to preserve her son's life (another rugged return journey of at least 400 kms) – back to Nazareth – growing realization of her Son's costly commission – learning to release Him to God's purposes – these and many more hurdles she had to face. Yet she walked through them without complaining, treasuring precious memories in her heart. (Luke 2:19).

Separation: The tender mother-son relationship was there to the end when Jesus committed His mother to John's care (John 19:25-27). Yet Jesus seemed to be gently pressing her to see that SPIRITUAL FIDELITY must PREDOMINATE over HUMAN RELATIONSHIPS. The first hint of this was in the temple incident. (Luke 2:49 & 50: 'Didn't you know I had to be in My Father's house?' NIV) Then there was the mild reproof at the wedding in Cana. (John 2:4: 'Woman, what have I to do with you?') Later, Jesus clearly teaches 'Whoever does God's will is thy brother and sister and mother.' (Mark 3:31-35). Finally, teaching on discipleship in Luke 14:26-27 He says 'If anyone comes to Me and does not hate ... (i.e. put human relationships in right perspective) ... he cannot be My disciple.' Mary was being prepared in spirit for the big change which lay ahead.

A New Relationship: No mother's heart can fail to identify in some measure with Mary as she became a helpless witness to His persecution, unjust trial and crucifixion. The human desolation must have been overwhelming. Did doubt creep in? Had God failed?

Then all the suffering was swept aside. The good news rang out: 'He is not here. He is risen.' Prayerfully, expectantly Mary joined the others to await the coming of the Spirit (Acts 1:14). She was now part of the living, growing, witnessing, fearless, rejoicing Church pressing on in the certain hope of His coming again (Acts 1:11).

Just a Woman: Mary – the village girl, an ordinary woman, a drawer of water, a dependable mother and exemplary wife, proving God in the ordinary (and very extraordinary!) warp and woof of daily living. Yet she personified all the traits of Christian character which any Christian woman should covet ... Humility (Luke 1:48-52), spiritual mindedness (Luke 2:51), model mother (Luke 2:51-52), full of faith and piety (Luke 1:46-55), submissive (Luke 1:38), sensitive to God (Luke 1:29-30). Surely Elizabeth's words sum it all up – 'Blessed are you among women, blessed is the Child you will bear.'

This can be our portion to if we walk in submissive co-operation with Christ. We can live to 'magnify the Lord' (Luke 1:46). Like the virtuous woman in Proverbs it can be said of us.

> 'Her children arise and call her blessed'
> Her husband also, and he praises her.' (Prov. 31:28).

STUDY 3

ANNA – THE MINISTRY OF PRAYER AND FASTING

QUESTIONS

DAY 1 *Luke 2:36; Exodus 15:20; Judges 4:4; 2 Kings 22:14.*

a) We are told that Anna was a prophetess. What do you understand by that term?

b) Do you know of any other Bible women who are in that category?

DAY 2 *Luke 2:36, 37; 1 Thessalonians 4:13-18; Isaiah 61:1-3; James 1:27.*

Anna suffered widowhood after only seven years of marriage. Give your thoughts on how we can find comfort when faced with bereavement. Share your own experiences if this applies.

DAY 3 a) Compare Luke 2:37 with Paul's command 'Pray without ceasing' in 1 Thessalonians 5:17. Discuss how this is possible.

b) Name some of the great pray-ers of the Bible.

c) Contrast the prayers of the Pharisees (Luke 18:9-12; Matt. 6:5; Mark 12:40) with those of some of these great pray-ers. Consider Ezra 9, Nehemiah 1, Daniel 9, Exodus 32:11-13, 30-32.

DAY 4 a) Is fasting relevant today? (Look up some New Testament passages such as Matt. 4:2; 6:16-18; 9:14-15; 17:21 [AV]; Acts 10:30 [AV].)

b) What are some occasions that call for prayer and fasting, and what results may be seen? Let members of the group share any experiences they may have heard about or shared in.

DAY 5 a) Remember how later Jesus cleansed that same temple of those who were defiling it (Matt. 21:12, 13). What is the temple a picture of for us (I Cor. 6:19, 20)?

b) How can we be guilty of defiling it?

DAY 6 a) Anna gave thanks to God because she had seen the Saviour. Why have we who are Christians still more reason to give thanks to God?

b) What are some effects of praise in our lives? Consider Nehemiah 8:10; Philippians 4:6, 7; 2 Chronicles 20:15-22; Psalm 149:6-9; Ephesians 5:18-20.

c) Think of Bible characters who in spite of suffering, had developed an attitude of thanking and praising God: Matthew 26:26, 27; Psalm 18:1-3; Jonah 2:9; Acts 16:25-34; Revelation 7:10-14. In what kind of sufferings did they praise God?

NOTE: Other Bible words akin to 'thanks' are 'praise', 'worship', 'rejoice', 'hope'. These all add up to developing a positive attitude to life, because of God's love and faithfulness towards us.

DAY 7 *Luke 2:38.*

a) What new ministry did Anna have after God's revelation to her that Jesus was the promised Redeemer?

b) Can you think of another woman who was privileged to be the first witness of Jesus' resurrection? (John 20:17, 18).

c) John 20:21; Mark 16:15, 16; Acts 1:8; Acts 13:3; 2 Corinthians 5:19, 20. In the light of these verses, why should we become witnesses for Jesus?

NOTES

There are many 'saints in service' such as Anna, whose biographies are fragmentary. How we would like to know more about the life of this remarkable woman but perhaps we can use our imagination to fill in a few gaps.

Apparently Anna's ancestors on their return from captivity in Assyria had settled hack in Israel. There Anna was brought up by her mother and father, Phanuel, who was of the tribe of Asher. Like every other girl she looked forward to a happy marriage, but her happiness was short lived. Seven years after her marriage Anna was widowed. Such sadness causes some to go through the rest of their lives full of self-pity. Others find that such a heartbreak drives them into a deeper relationship with God. Such was the case with Anna.

Very little is said about Anna's parentage. No doubt her home background had some bearing on her decision, as a young widow to devote herself wholly to the service of the Lord. Her father's name, Phanuel, means 'face of God'. That would indicate either that he was godly in character or a man who sought God's face in prayer – or both. If this was so, then Anna's life and future decisions would have been shaped by this godly influence and example. Anna's own name means 'Grace'.

Eventually, it seems, she took up residence in the living quarters of the temple, where she spent her time waiting on God. He brought her into an intimate relationship with Himself, in which she began to receive revelations from God, and became known by all as a prophetess. He showed her that the Redeemer was soon to appear.

Slipping quietly in, then out of this account in Luke chapter 2 is Simeon – a devout and godly soul who frequented the Temple. He lived in the hope of the coming Messiah. God had revealed to him that he would not die before the Promised One came. Had Anna learned from him? They were definitely kindred spirits in this realm of expectant hope. Their simultaneous affirmation of Jesus as the Christ rings forth with clarity – Simeon's in verses 29-35 and Anna's in verse 38. It is hardly to be wondered at, if the discerning Anna was prayerfully burdened for Temple priests who lived in hypocrisy and heartlessness (Matt. 23:27-34), that she would rejoice in the quality of spiritual encouragement which Simeon obviously offered.

From the statement 'she did not depart from the temple, but worshipped with fasting and prayers night and day', three words stand out – 'worship, fasting, prayers'. We are not to understand that Anna spent twenty-four hours a day on her knees. No, Anna did her shopping and housework and other chores as we do. But she had learned the secret of remaining in a spirit of communion with God continually, sometimes fasting from meals when God laid special burdens on her heart.

And then it happened. One day when Anna was eighty-four years old, she felt an urge to go into the temple. There before her was the familiar sight of a young couple who had brought their baby to dedicate to the Lord. Suddenly her heart leaped for joy as God revealed to her that this baby was the promised Messiah. Anna placed a trembling wrinkled old hand on the baby's head, and offered up a sincere prayer of thanksgiving to God.

From then until the day of her death Anna had a new ministry. There was a new light in her eyes as she began to tell those who came to worship God, 'The Redeemer has come. He is still a baby. But my eyes have seen Him. Prepare your hearts for He will appear and you must be ready.' First the shepherds, then the wise men, then old Simeon and Anna had become God's messengers to proclaim the Saviour, even before John the Baptist announced His coming. But let us remember that the revelations God gave to Anna came as a result of hours spent in waiting on God, with her spiritual ear attuned to hear His voice.

Prayer is a neglected ministry in this generation. Search the scriptures and discover God's directive to us about prayer. For those who carve out time alone with God there are physical, spiritual, personal and general benefits. They that wait on the Lord exchange strength (Isa. 40:31). The secret of fruitful ministry and witness is a consistent, persistent, private seeking of God's face in prayer. (e.g. Mark 9:29; Col. 4:2; Rev. 5:8 and many more!)

STUDY 4

MARTHA – PRACTICAL SPIRITUALITY!

QUESTIONS

DAY 1 *Luke 10:38-42; 1 Peter 4:9; Philippians 4:6, 7.*

a) How did both sisters meet Jesus' needs?

b) Discuss the drawbacks in the temperaments of the two sisters.

c) Martha was preparing a special meal for Jesus. What two faults do we see in her attitude? Discuss ways in which we might show the same faults.

DAY 2 *John 11:1-5; 15:9; 1 Peter 5:7.*

a) What event drew the sisters into a greater oneness?

b) What was Jesus' attitude to all three members of the family?

c) How does the statement in John 11:5 encourage us?

DAY 3 *John 11:6-10; 1 Peter 5:7.*

a) Why do you suppose Jesus stayed two days longer?

b) What do we learn from the differing attitudes of Jesus and His disciples?

c) Put verses 9 and 10 into your own words.

DAY 4 *John 11:17-27; 1 Thessalonians 4:13-18.*

a) What do verses 21 and 22 tell us of Martha's faith?

b) Martha had faith for the future rather than for the present. How may we also show this same attitude?

c) What tremendous revelation of Himself did Jesus make to Martha? How can this be a comfort to us today?

d) Martha's further declaration of faith (v. 27) equals that of another disciple. Who was he? (Matt. 16:16).

DAY 5 *John 11:28-37; Isaiah 55:9.*

a) How does Martha show concern for her younger sister?

b) How did the first words both sisters spoke to Jesus reveal what they had been saying together during those four sorrowful days?

DAY 6 *John 11:38-44; 5:24-29.*

a) How did Martha see the glory of God?

b) What do you feel was Jesus' motive in raising Lazarus to life?

DAY 7 *John 12:1, 2.*

a) How can we follow the example of Martha's special ministry?

b) Is showing hospitality a ministry for all, or an optional extra? (Rom. 12:13; Heb. 13:2).

NOTES

A haven for Jesus and His disciples

The home at Bethany was two miles from Jerusalem. Jesus found a welcome there and frequently visited it. From the gospel narrative we discover He went from Bethany to the Last Supper and His betrayal. The Bethany family obviously loved Him and the two women readily attended to His needs when He was a guest there. Hospitable Martha was prone to panic, just like you or I would, when thirteen tired and hungry men arrived on her doorstep.

The family team

Little is said of Lazarus, but we do learn quite a bit about the character of the two women. Martha means 'lady' or 'mistress'. As the elder sister she obviously took responsibility for domestic affairs. Mary, a good listener, spontaneously spent time with her guests. It seems to me this could have been a very harmonious teamship as they entertained, had it not been for pressures which 'got to' Martha.

Temperaments

The Lord has made us all so different and for good reason. Both these women were devoted to Jesus and would have done anything for His comfort. Mary's 'listening' disposition indicates she was sympathetic and understanding, eager to learn from Him and preferred to put spiritual before material needs. Dear, practical Martha, totally aware of the Master's need of physical refreshment got busy preparing a first-class meal. What went wrong? Was she not as well organized as usual? Was the fire refusing to burn? Anyway, she got 'all het up' and under the pressure took it out on her (idle?) sister. It is a fact of life, both in home and family affairs, that the quiet contemplative 'Marys' and the bustling, practical 'Marthas' do 'get in each other's hair'! The answer to the problem is to develop an awareness of each other's needs and seek to fit in. 'Marys' have to learn to be more practically helpful. 'Marthas' need to get priorities into focus – perhaps prepare simpler food and thus leave more time for the most important side of life. It is good to know Jesus understands each of us, loves us and patiently teaches us to be more like Him. Martha was familiar enough with Jesus to take her problem to Him. Sometimes we suffer (and make others suffer too!) because we don't live close enough to Him or are too slow to share our frustrations with Him.

Calamity

Jesus had failed the Bethany family. He had not come in time. Lazarus was dead. Both the sisters exercised faith to the extent that they KNEW Jesus. He could have HEALED Lazarus of sickness. Now it was too late! Little did they know what Jesus was about to do. Martha had run to meet Jesus on the way. As she told Him of the hopelessness of the situation she typified our human reactions and lack of spiritual perception at times of crisis. But Scripture encourages us to look beyond our circumstances and put our faith in Him, like Peter in Matthew 14:25-31. Jesus is equal to the situation even when the odds seem impossibly against us.

Revelation and Confession
Listen to the dialogue between Martha and Jesus:

Martha	'It's too late. Lazarus is dead.'
Jesus	'Your brother will rise again.'
Martha	'I know he will, in the resurrection at the last day.'
Jesus	'I AM the RESURRECTION and the LIFE.'
Martha	'I BELIEVE that YOU are the CHRIST, the SON of GOD, Who was to come.

What a wonderful REVELATION had come to Martha's heart. She was able to CONFESS her faith in the Son of God BEFORE He performed the miracle of Resurrection.

Comfort
Then Martha went to Mary. 'The Teacher is here and wants you.' Jesus fully identifies with the two sisters and their mourning friends. He weeps with them – deeply moved in His Spirit and troubled (John 11:33). Mary, in her grief, knew solace.

Human Reasoning and Divine Assurance
Martha was again overcome by her practical nature as they arrived at the sealed tomb of Lazarus. 'It's hopeless, Lord. His body is rotting. What's the use of opening the grave?' Oh Martha. Don't you remember His words? 'If you believe you will see the glory of God' (John 11:40).

Resurrection
'Lazarus, come out!' The dead man came out.
'Take off the grave-clothes and let him go.'

Scripture makes no comment on Martha's reactions. As Christ's words were fulfilled and Lazarus stood before her alive and well, her heart must have been bursting with joy and praise to God. Over and over again as she watched Lazarus around the home the truth must have been echoing in her heart 'I am the Resurrection and the Life.' This 'faith boosting' miracle, this vivid 'audio visual' must have encouraged the disciples and friends of Jesus as they watched Him suffer, die and being laid in the tomb. The same words must have re-echoed in their hearts when the glad news was brought to them on the Resurrection morning 'He is not here, He is risen.'

Points to ponder:
Death holds no terror for those who have put their trust in the RESURRECTED SON OF GOD. Read 1 Corinthians 15:51-55. Death has been swallowed up in victory (v. 54) and those who are Christians can say:

'Where, O death, is your victory?
'Where, O death, is your sting?' (v. 55)

STUDY 5

MARY MAGDALENE - MINISTRY OF WITNESSING

QUESTIONS

DAY 1 a) Can you give examples of people who have been delivered from evil spirits? (Luke 8:1-3; Matt. 17:18; Acts 16:16-18).

b) Who has the supreme authority over Satan? (1 John 3:8; Matt. 28:18).

c) To whom does Jesus give authority to cast out evil powers today? (Luke 9:1; 10:1, 17-19; Mark 16:17).

DAY 2 *Luke 8:1-3, Matthew 25:40; 1 Peter 4:8-10.*
a) How did Mary and the other women show their gratitude to Jesus?

b) Can we show our gratitude in a similar way today?

DAY 3 *John 19:25-27: Mark 15:40, 41; Matthew 27:55-61.*
a) Mary Magdalene was at the cross, not only to show love to Jesus but to support someone else in her grief. Who was that?

b) Do you find that sharing grief draws people together? Can you think of other biblical instances?

c) It would have been an agonizing experience for the women to see Jesus crucified. What does their presence there show of their character?

DAY 4 *Matthew 28:1; Mark 16:1-3; John 20:1; Luke 23:55–24:1.*

a) What service did Mary Magdalene and the other woman wish to do for Jesus?

b) What was their dilemma as they approached the tomb?

c) What does the friendship of this group of women teach us?

DAY 5 *Matthew 28:1-8; Luke 24:1-11. (NOTE: The accounts in the four Gospels do not contradict each other, but together give us a complete picture.)*

a) Why should the women, as well as the disciples, have expected that Jesus would rise again? (Matt. 28:6; Luke 24:6-8.)

b) Why did the angel roll back the stone in front of the tomb?

c) Compare the attitude of the women with that of the apostles to the angel's message (Luke 24; Mark 16:9, 10, 14).

DAY 6 *John 20:11-18*

a) Why do you think Mary was still weeping after the angels had already told her that Jesus was alive? (Matt. 28:6).

b) How does she refer to Jesus in her conversation with the angels? Can you refer to Him in the same terms?

c) Which verse tells us that Mary, out of love for Jesus, would attempt an almost impossible task?

DAY 7 *John 20:11-18; Mark 16:9; Acts 1:8.*

a) Why did Mary not recognize Jesus immediately?

b) What caused her to recognize Him?

c) Can you personalize this incident, hearing Jesus tenderly call you by name? What would your reply be?

d) Mary wanted to hold Jesus, but Jesus wanted her to learn she must now share Him. How did she do that? How can we?

NOTES

The Power of Evil

Nothing is known of the background of Mary who came from the village of Magdala on the shore of the Sea of Galilee. Whether her family had been involved in evil practices or Mary herself had dabbled in the occult is a matter of conjecture. We are well warned in the Bible to steer clear of divination, magic, necromancy, sorcery and witchcraft. It is the devil's delight to snare even Christians into seemingly 'harmless' activities such as fortune telling, Ouija board, horoscopes, palmistry, tea-leaf reading which are really his tactics to get fuller footholds in our lives. Many people are deliberately moving into witchcraft and worship of the devil in this generation. Whatever Mary Magdalene's involvement, evil spirits had a strong grip on her mind and she lived in a state of torment, terror and despair till Jesus came to her village.

The Power of God

One authoritative word from Jesus released Mary from her living hell and banished forever these seven evil spirits. (Mark 16:9; Luke 8:2 etc). Mary was healed, transformed, and the whole course of her life changed.

The Bible tells us clearly that Jesus came to destroy the works of the devil. (1 John 3:8). The devil sought to destroy Jesus (Luke 4:2-13), but Christ overcame him (Rev. 3:21) and we can overcome through Him (1 John 2:13). Yet we are warned not to give the devil a foothold in our lives (Eph. 4:27), to be vigilant against his devices (1 Pet. 5:8), and to resist him (1 Pet. 5:9). The devil cannot undo God's work of saving grace in our lives, but he schemes to make us disobedient, defeated, ineffective witnesses. He cannot come where Jesus reigns supreme – so we are safe when we walk close to Him and give Him full rein in our lives.

Devoted Follower

That is how Mary started to live. Out of her love and gratitude for all He had done for her she 'kept company with Jesus'. She joined the Galilean women who accompanied Jesus and the disciples, probably washing, mending and cooking for them (Mark 15:41). Mary 'kept company' with Jesus till the end of His life on earth thrilled to see the throngs crowding to Him for help and teaching – perplexed and torn as she sensed mounting opposition – empathizing as He was mocked, tried and condemned – agonizing through His ordeal on the cross (John 19:28) – grieving deeply as she followed with Joseph and Nicodemus to the grave (Matt. 27:61). Probably it was only the presence of the guard that forced her ultimately to give up her vigil at the tomb.

Discovery

When Mary and her companions arrived at the tomb in the early morning to anoint the body of Jesus, they were taken by surprise. The earth shook as an angel of the Lord descended from heaven, rolled back the stone and sat on it. The guards fainted with fear but the angel said to the women, 'Do not be afraid, for I know that you are looking for Jesus, Who was crucified. He is not here; He has risen, just as He said. Come and see the place where He lay. Then go quickly and tell the disciples: '"He is risen from the dead and is going ahead of you into Galilee. There you will see Him." Now I have told you' (Matt 28:1-7). Can you imagine how swiftly Mary went to bear the news? Peter and John went with her, saw the empty tomb and returned home. But Mary remained, no doubt struggling between faith and fear. Her pent-up emotions found expression in tears – then Jesus came, just as He had done in the first place, and met her in her need.

Revelation

'Mary!' 'Master!' The doubts disappeared. She knew His voice! Jesus had risen. Her living Lord had spoken – to her personally! So Mary Magdalene was the FIRST to see Him, the FIRST commissioned by Him. She was FIRST at the tomb and her vigilance was rewarded. Her heart must have been bursting with joy as she sped, for the second time with these words from the lips of Jesus Himself.

'I have seen the Lord. He said, "Go and tell"...' (John 20:10-18).

A New Relationship

Jesus had taken time to teach His mother, Mary, that an eternal, spiritual relationship must supersede the former human, earthly bonds. Now He imparted this truth to Mary Magdalene. 'Do not hold on to Me, for I have not yet returned to my Father. Go instead to my brothers and tell them, "I am returning to MY Father and YOUR Father, to MY God and YOUR God."' From then on Mary came to know Christ, not after the flesh, but after the Spirit (2 Cor. 5:16, 17).

Christ has finished His atoning work (John 19:30)
He has risen from the dead (Rom. 1:4)
He has ascended to the Father (Acts 5:31)
He intercedes constantly for us (Rom. 8:34)
He has entrusted the task, not only to Mary (John 20:17)
but to all His children (Matt. 28:18-20)
to 'Go and tell'
What a tremendous privilege!

It should be our JOY and DELIGHT to spread the Good News.

STUDY 6

BARNABAS – THE CONSTANT ENCOURAGER

QUESTIONS

DAY 1 *Acts 4:32-37; James 2:14-20.*

a) What conclusions would you draw about the spiritual life of these early Christians from the practices they adopted?

b) Is the level of your generosity a true reflection of your spiritual life?

DAY 2 *Acts 9:23-31.*

a) 'Barnabas' means, 'son of encouragement'. What, do you feel caused Barnabas to be of help to Paul? Can you think of someone in your circle who is needing a bit of encouragement?

b) What were the practical results of Paul's spiritual turn about and bold proclamation of the gospel? (see v. 31).

DAY 3 *Acts 11:19-26.*

a) What factors do you think influenced the church at Jerusalem to choose Barnabas for the Antioch assignment?

b) What prompted Barnabas to get Paul to help him in the teaching of the new Antiochan converts? (Are you tackling some bit of service on your own, when God might want you to enlist some help?)

DAY 4 *Acts 11:29, 30; 12:24, 25; 13:1-5.*

a) In this early instance of missionary outreach, a group of leaders in the church were led to send out two of their number. Today it is usually the individual who volunteers to go, rather than the church taking the initiative to send out. Which pattern is right?

b) Which activity (or non-activity!) is mentioned twice in verses 2 and 3? What do you consider is the objective?

c) Why do you think Paul and Barnabas went to Cyprus? (See 4:36, 37.)

DAY 5 *Acts 14:8-15; 19-22.*

a) What contrast in treatment did Paul and Barnabas receive in Lystra?

b) Does this discourage or encourage you? Why?

c) What must have influenced Paul and Barnabas to return to Lystra (v. 21)? What was the reward? (see 16:1.)

DAY 6 *Acts 15:1, 2, 22-29.*

a) The council at Jerusalem decided to send a letter to the churches containing the findings of their deliberations. They sent it by Paul and Barnabas. What qualifications did they have for such a bit of service? Would this strengthen the impact of the message?

b) 'It seemed good to the Holy Spirit and to us' (v. 28). What can you learn from this quaint phrase?

DAY 7 *Acts 15:36-41.*

a) Paul and Barnabas had a sharp clash over John Mark's suitability for further missionary service. What was Paul's reason for not wanting to take him (v. 38)? Who was proved right in the end? (See 2 Tim. 4:11 – written towards the end of Paul's life.)

b) What happens to you when you can't agree with another Christian? What should happen?

c) What is the major lesson that has come through to you from this week's study?

NOTES

What a magnificent person we have studied this week! He is foremost of all the New Testament missionaries in the priceless ministry of *encouragement.* In fact his name means 'son of encouragement'.

Let us take a look at a few situations in which this gift took a prominent position.

1. *Acts 9:27.*

Paul – hitherto a persecutor of Christians – was a new convert, needing fellowship and help. The Christians were suspicious and didn't accept him, but Barnabas did. He *trusted* Paul; he *encouraged* him; he *befriended* him; he *spoke up* for him when he took him to the apostles.

2. *Acts 11:19.*

Many had come to the Lord in the town of Antioch. When the news reached Jerusalem the Christians thought, 'Whom can we send to help and encourage and teach these new converts?' The answer was – Barnabas! True enough when he got there he embarked on an encouraging and supporting ministry (v. 23).

3. *Acts 13:43-51.*

Here we find Barnabas and Paul in another Antioch – this time a town in Asia Minor. The preaching of the gospel in the synagogue had created a cleavage – many rejecting the message, but many receiving it and wanting to know more. What did Paul and Barnabas do in this situation? We read that they 'persuaded them to continue in the grace of God' (v. 43). In fact they abandoned any idea of staying with the rejecting Jews and instead saw their commission as being for the encouragement of Gentiles (vv. 46, 47).

4. *Acts 15:36-41.*

Since John Mark had deserted Paul and Barnabas during their first missionary journey (13:13) Paul was determined not to take him on a second journey. Barnabas however felt just as strongly that he should be given another chance. Of course some would say, 'Blood is thicker than water and since Mark was his cousin he was batting for him.' But it goes further. Barnabas, the encourager was determined to do all he could to help Mark make the grade. Who proved to be right? Not Paul but Barnabas, because later Paul says in a letter to Timothy, 'Mark is a useful worker.' And of course we have the Gospel of Mark to prove it.

Barnabas was a native of Cyprus and the beginning of his attachment to the Christian community is marked by an act of sacrifice – he donated money from the sale of his land holdings to the common purse (4:37) in line with early practice (2:45). Our handling of finance is a pretty good thermometer on the warmth of our devotion!

STUDY 7

MARK

QUESTIONS

DAY 1 *Acts 12:5-16.*

a) Why do you think Peter headed for the home of Mary, Mark's mother?

b) What effect do you think Peter's arrival had on the young Mark?

c) Is there a place for home prayer meetings?

DAY 2 *Acts 12:25-13:5.*

a) Mark was apparently 'apprenticed' to Paul and Barnabas. Jesus trained his disciples in 'on the spot' situations. What do you think was behind this?

b) How was the decision to send out the first missionaries made?

c) Today we expect individuals to 'volunteer'. Which method is best?

DAY 3 *Acts 13:13; 15:36-41.*

a) Paul resisted Barnabas's proposal to take Mark on the second journey. Was he justified in doing so?

b) What lesson can be learned from Mark's failure? (see 2 Tim. 4:11). Can you look back to a past failure? Have you learned anything from it?

DAY 4 *2 Timothy 4:11; Colossians 4:10; I Peter 5:13.*

a) What do these verses, plus the existence of the Gospel of Mark, tell us about John Mark?

b) What do you think Mark's special gift was (I Pet. 4:10)?

DAY 5 *Acts 13:13-16, 28-52.*

a) What valuable lessons could John Mark have learned if he had stayed with Paul and Barnabas through these experiences?

b) Although Paul was a Jew, God was sending him to the Gentiles (see v. 47 and 26:17). Why?

DAY 6 *Mark 9:14-29.*

This is a sample of Mark's writing which we will contrast with Matthew's and Luke's tomorrow. Meanwhile, what could a Christian servant learn from this passage about a) faith, and b) prayer?

DAY 7 *Read Matthew 17:14-21 and Luke 9:37-42 and compare them with Mark's account of the same incident in yesterday's portion.*

a) Who gives the most detail?

b) Whose account is the most colourful?

c) Whose account helps us to understand the thoughts and attitudes of the participants?

d) What is the final impression that you gain from this week's study?

NOTES

We drop in on a drop-out!

So you don't think much of yourself? Tendency to come under condemnation? Join the John Mark club! But you'll be interested to know he didn't found it! It started with Abraham. Later Moses was in it for a while, then David and Jonah. Peter was also a member for a period. They were all failures at a certain point in their lives. *But they didn't stay failures!* And that's the big lesson of John Mark's life.

Some scholars feel that the first reference to Mark is in Mark's Gospel 14:51, where he is identified as the young man who ran off naked rather than be taken as a follower of Jesus. So the streaker became a sticker!

He must have had a fairly wealthy home because it was big enough for groups of Christians to gather for prayer. It was in fact to his home that Peter immediately went after being led out of prison (Acts 12). His father is never mentioned and as the house is described as 'Mary's', it is reasonable to assume he was dead.

John went as an attendant or helper to Barnabas and Paul on their first missionary journey from Antioch (Acts 13:5). But something must have happened when they were in Cyprus – the first area tackled. As soon as the three got back to the mainland Mark left them and went home. This departure was obviously seen as a failure by Paul, because when considering a second journey (Acts 15:38) he refused point blank to have Mark with him.

Barnabas, true to his reputation as an encourager, was determined to give him another opportunity to prove the Lord, so the two key figures separated over their opinion of Mark. Of course it must be noted that Barnabas would have known him more intimately because he was his cousin, and also Barnabas was a Cypriot and perhaps understood more than Paul some of the factors leading to Mark's failure on that island.

At any rate, Paul later changed his mind because he says in his last letter to Timothy that Mark is a useful worker (2 Tim. 4:11). And of course we have Mark's magnificent Gospel as a further proof of his spiritual growth.

Only a few other references to Mark occur in the New Testament. One is Colossians 4:10 where he is mentioned as in the company of Paul (so they must have been reconciled by then). He is also mentioned in Philemon 24 along with other workers, notably Luke.

From I Peter 5:13 we gather that there was a close relationship between Mark and Peter. Indeed it might be reasonably assumed that Peter was Mark's spiritual father. Tradition has it that most of the material of Mark's Gospel comes from eyewitness accounts that Peter gave to Mark – accounts that were graphic, detailed and fast moving.

STUDY 8

TIMOTHY – STIMULUS FOR THE FAINT-HEARTED

QUESTIONS

DAY 1 *Acts 16:1; John 13:35; 15:5-8; Luke 14:27; John 8:31.*

a) Timothy is described as a 'disciple'. Study how Jesus defines a disciple in the references given and compile your own definition. (How do you rate yourself in the light of this?)

b) Why does Jesus bring such an emphasis on discipleship rather than just majoring on the need to be 'born again'?

DAY 2 *Acts 16:1-5.*

a) What do you think were the factors that induced Paul to take Timothy with him?

b) What happened to Paul on a previous visit to Lystra? (See 14:6, 7, 19-21.) Can you see something precious about the fact that Paul found his best co-worker there?

DAY 3 *Acts 16:1-18.*

a) Imagine you are Timothy and having left home you go through the experiences described here, with Paul. What are some of the lessons you might have learned?

b) Why did God hinder Paul and his companions from going to Mysia, Asia and Bithynia, when there were needy people there?

DAY 4 *Philippians 2:19-24.*

a) Paul obviously thinks very highly of Timothy as a co-worker. For what reasons? Can you learn anything from this?

b) Why did Paul want to send Timothy to the church at Philippi?

c) What does this reveal about Paul's attitude? (Is this a pointer for you in your attitude to younger Christians?)

DAY 5 *I Corinthians 16:10, 11; I Timothy 5:23; 4:12; 2 Timothy 1:4, 6, 7.*

a) What image is conjured up in your mind after reading these verses about Timothy? Bear in mind Paul's words in I Corinthians 1:27, 28.

b) What does this do for you?

c) Regarding 2 Timothy 1:6, what is your spiritual gift? Is it being used consistently or does it need 'stirring up' like Timothy's? (see I Pet. 4:10 for proof that you have one!)

DAY 6 *2 Timothy 1:1-7; 3:15.*

a) What does this passage tell us about Timothy's background? (Refer also to Acts 16:1)

b) Where does the primary responsibility for the training of children in Christian truth lie? (See also Eph. 6:4.)

DAY 7 *2 Timothy 2:1-4; 4:2, 5.*

a) From 2:2 what pattern do you see for the training of disciples? Are you fulfilling your part? (In whom are you investing?)

b) Paul uses the picture of a soldier to describe the qualities of a true disciple. What qualities are there? (see also I Tim. 1:18).

NOTES

What a limited person Timothy was! Yet how God used him! If anyone doing this study is given to having a low self-image, here is your patron saint! Note that he was:

a. *Fearful* (2 Tim. 1:7) yet entrusted with encouraging the Thessalonians to be brave in the face of persecution – See 1 Thessalonians 3:2, 3.

b. *Lacking force of character* (1 Cor. 16:10; 2 Tim. 2:1), yet sent to 'sort out' a divided church (1 Cor. 4:17).

c. *In indifferent health* (1 Tim. 5:23) yet Paul commended him for the concern and burden he had for others (Phil. 2:19-21).

d. *Limited by lack of experience* (1 Tim. 4:12), yet entrusted with straightening out those who were going astray in their doctrine (1 Tim. 1:3, 4).

e. *Lacking in emotional stability* (2 Tim. 1:4; 2 Tim. 2:22-23), yet given responsibility to ensure that others maintained a steady walk in the Lord (2 Tim. 2:24-26).

f. *Conscious of his natural limitations* (1 Tim. 4:14; 2 Tim. 1:6), yet expected to be a good example to others (1 Tim. 4:12).

g. *Probably reticent in asserting his own convictions* (2 Tim. 1:8), yet was given the task of teaching others and refuting false teachers (1 Tim. 1 :3-4; 4:6, 8).

Timothy was God's reward to Paul for his indefatigable determination to keep on returning to Lystra, the place of maximum opposition, in order to see Christians established in the faith (Acts 14:19, 21, 22; 16:1).

Although his father was Greek, his mother and grandmother were Jewish Christians (2 Tim. 1:5) and they ensured that he had a good grounding in the Old Testament Scriptures (2 Tim. 3:15). This of course predisposed him to be sensitive to the life-giving message of the gospel, and his early growth in spiritual things was noted by other local Christians (Acts 16:2).

Paul saw his potential and invited him to accompany him and Silas. If Mark hadn't proved a failure and gone with Barnabas because of Paul's refusal to take him again, Timothy would probably not have been needed. Interesting! (Rom. 8:28).

His circumcision – though quite unnecessary (Gal. 5:6) – had one objective, namely that in the evangelizing of other Jews he would be culturally more acceptable to them.

It is clear that Paul had a very high appreciation of Timothy's faithful service and that Timothy was a selfless and totally dedicated worker who placed others' needs away ahead of his own (Phil. 2:19-22).

Apart from being Paul's companion on numerous journeys, we gather from many references that he had some important responsibilities which he had to shoulder at various times:

a. He was sent to Thessalonica to minister to the Christians and strengthen their faith in the midst of persecution and discouragement (1 Thess. 3:1-6).

b. He shared in the church planting ministry at Corinth (2 Cor. 1:19).

c. He was commissioned by Paul to go from Ephesus to the Corinthian church so that he could have a stabilizing ministry, helping them to apply and appropriate spiritual principles to some problem situations.

d. He pastored the Ephesian church for a time, and in view of the prevalence of erroneous doctrines, was encouraged by Paul to maintain a strong teaching ministry designed to stabilize the Christians, and to deal effectively with false teachers (I Tim. 1:3-7).

He was also responsible for seeing that the church was properly constituted by the appointment of suitable elders and deacons.

It appears that at one stage he spent a period in jail (Heb. 13:23).

STUDY 9

AQUILA AND PRISCILLA
EPAPHRAS

QUESTIONS

AQUILA AND PRISCILLA - THE MINISTRY OF HOSPITALITY

DAY 1 *Acts 18:1-11.*

a) Paul had a special affinity with Aquila and Priscilla. Should you use your occupation as a bridge for the gospel?

b) Paul's experience highlights the problem of how to handle those who resist the gospel. Does his action establish a precedent for us in our witnessing?

DAY 2 *Acts 18:18, 19, 24-28.*

a) As in yesterday's reading, Aquila's and Priscilla's home is mentioned as a place of lodging for Paul. Here we see it as a place of instruction for Apollos. Do you see your home as a strategic resource? How are you using it for God?

b) We also see from verses 18 and 19 that they were quite mobile. What does this highlight about their attitude to their home?

DAY 3 *Romans 16:3-5; 1 Corinthians 16:19.*

a) What more can we learn about how Aquila and Priscilla used their home?

b) Aquila and Priscilla obviously had earned a reputation by this time. How do they contrast with Ananias and Sapphira in Acts 5:1-5?

DAY 4 *Reread all the portions of this week, plus 2 Timothy 4:19.*

a) Did you notice that whenever Aquila is mentioned Priscilla is mentioned also? What does this indicate?

b) Look up these references to homes in the New Testament – Acts 12:12; 16:15, 32; 18:3, 11, 26, 27; Colossians 4:15; Philemon 2. Summarize all the ways that you feel a home can be used for God.

DAY 5 *Reread Romans 16:4 in connection with 2 Timothy 2:3 and Luke 14:27.*
a) True discipleship seems to point to a lifestyle that involves ... what?

b) Evaluate the degree of hardship, loss, risk and sacrifice that your service for Christ involves. Are you a real New Testament Christian?

EPAPHRAS - THE INTERCESSOR

DAY 6 *Colossians 1:7; 4:12, 13.*
a) Pick out the phrases used to describe the way Epaphras carried out his ministry and summarize these in your own words.

b) Epaphras is described as wrestling or striving in prayer. What level of intensity does your prayer life have?

DAY 7 *1 Timothy 2:1-4; Exodus 32:30-32 (start at verse 1 if you want the full story).*
a) Note the four levels of prayer in 1 Timothy 2:1. The deepest is intercession – when we take responsibility for another's need. Moses is an example. Epaphras is another (Col. 4:12). What objectives did the intercession of Epaphras have?

b) See Romans 1:9; Philippians 1:4; Colossians 1:9; 1 Thessalonians 1:2, 3. Here we see Paul continuously interceding for the churches, just as Epaphras was doing for the Colossians. Have you accepted an intercessory responsibility for anyone? Why not pray about your prayer life?

NOTES

AQUILA AND PRISCILLA

Here is the happy, hospitable, husband-and-wife team.

Meet Mr. and Mrs Eagle (that's what 'Aquila' means in Latin), the unique husband-and-wife team of the early church. In all the New Testament references to them the one is never mentioned without the other. They were leather workers (eastern tents were made of animal skins), and the first report of them indicates that they had a ministry of *hospitality.*

(This week's study will ask you to do some serious thinking about using your home for the Lord).

Apparently they had to get out of Rome when Jews were being persecuted, so they moved to Corinth and that's where they met Paul and gave him hospitality. Many Christians have been blessed through having Christian workers in their home – try it some time!

There is no mention of children in connection with Aquila and Priscilla. If they had none it would have been simpler for them to move with Paul than it would for parents. At any rate at his request they moved over to Ephesus with him.

It was here they again exercised a ministry of hospitality, this time to the itinerant preacher Apollos. Apparently his understanding of the gospel was limited and we read of both Aquila and Priscilla explaining salvation more fully to him. So they had a sufficient grasp of the truth to have something of a joint teaching ministry.

They were still at Ephesus when Paul wrote his first letter to the Corinthians (16:19) because he mentioned the church that was meeting in their home. This again indicates their readiness to make their home available to the Lord's people.

They must have moved back to Rome again because some time later, when writing to the Christians in Rome, Paul sent his greetings to Aquila and Priscilla (Rom. 16:3-5) and again mentioned the fact that they had established a Christian fellowship meeting in their home. In verse 4 of this passage we get a further glimpse of the quality of their life and witness. It seems that they really took risks in helping the Christians. So we see Aquila and Priscilla rendering sacrificial service, and although they were Jews by race offering this service to both Christian Jews and Gentiles alike. The gospel soon brings down racial barriers!

This week is a good one for Christian couples to ask themselves questions like these

1. Are we a team *together* in the work of the Lord?
2. Is our prayer life *together* vital and consistent and adequate?
3. Are we *together* using our home in the most effective way, for the gospel?
4. What is our type of 'witnessing' really costing us?
5. Are we willing to be mobile for God if He shows this to be His pattern?
6. Is our relationship to each other a good testimony?

EPAPHRAS

He knew what he was after!

We don't know much about Epaphras, but the little we do know is worth noting carefully. He is mentioned just three times, in Colossians 1:7, 4:12, and in Philemon 23.

From Colossians 1:7 we understand that it was through the ministry of Epaphras that the

Colossian Church had come into being. He was a church planter. There are not too many of these around today! The western church, by and large, does not have a 'planting' mentality, only a 'maintaining' one. Have you ever asked yourself why your church has never 'planted' another church? Having children is biologically natural! Having spiritual 'daughter churches' is thoroughly biblical!

The content of Colossians 4:12 is very telling. Here we have a glimpse of the church planter at prayer. He is one of God's intercessors, one who takes on the spiritual responsibility for others. A most interesting phrase is the one that says he is 'striving earnestly' in prayer for the Colossians. The Greek word is agonizomai – agonizing. The word comes from the root agon which was the Greek athletic contest when at a given signal all the competitors 'strained every nerve' in a maximum effort to be first. Another derivative – agonia – agony – is used in Luke 22:44 to describe the experience of the Lord Jesus in Gethsemane.

Are you playing at praying? Does the Lord want to bring you through to a new level of spiritual desire and intensity? It's not a matter of worked-up human feelings but of yielding to the constraint of the Holy Spirit. As Paul says in Colossians 1:29 (where the same word is used), he is 'striving' according to His energy which energizes him powerfully. 'Lord, teach us to *pray*!'

Behind one man's *maturity* is another's *agony!* See *Rees Howells, Intercessor* by Norman Grubb, (Lutterworth Press) for an account of a true intercessor.

STUDY 10

PHILIP – THE SENSITIVE SERVANT IN THE STRATEGY OF THE SPIRIT

QUESTIONS

DAY 1 *Acts 6:1-4.*

a) In a day when there was no welfare service, the care of widows was quite a crucial issue. Were the leaders (the 'twelve') justified in not becoming involved?

b) A racial or national distinction seems to have been part of the problem. Try to evaluate your personal attitude to people of a different colour. Do you *genuinely* consider them as equals?

DAY 2 Acts 6:1-7.

a) What qualifications did the men who were appointed need to have?

b) Think about the expression 'full of the Holy Spirit', and decide some of the practical implications of this description.

DAY 3 *Acts 8:4-13.*

a) 'It was a great tragedy that the Christians had to flee from Jerusalem.' What would you say to this? And what do you say to present day forms of persecution?

b) In your opinion why was Philip so greatly used in Samaria?

c) Do you want or expect God to use you? If so, what can you learn from this chapter?

DAY 4 *Acts 8:26-40.*

a) Do you think Philip had an inward struggle to leave all the wonderful happenings in Samaria? His instructions were vague, but everything worked out well. Why?

b) The Ethiopian had the Scriptures but he hadn't found Christ. What else did he need?

DAY 5 *Acts 8:26-40.*

a) Was the Ethiopian prepared for Philip's message? (How should this affect our prayers for people we are burdened about?)

b) How did Philip use the Scriptures?

c) Did Philip expect the Ethiopian to reach a decision? (When should we expect those we counsel to make a decision, and when shouldn't we?)

DAY 6 *Acts 11:5-15; 16:6-14.*

a) Compare the experience of Peter (Acts 11) and Paul (Acts 16) with that of Philip (yesterday's references). Can you see a pattern of God's dealings common to each?

b) What is the impact of these three stories on your level of concern for worldwide missions?

DAY 7 *Acts 21:8, 9.*

From Acts 8:40 we get the picture of Philip developing into an itinerant evangelist. During his subsequent experience he must have spent much time away from home. Yet we read some information here that commends him as a family man. Have you any comments?

NOTES

(Do not confuse this Philip with the disciple of the same name who became an apostle. John 1:43-46 and Acts 1:13.)

The few glimpses that we have of this man of God provide a challenge and an encouragement to sensitivity, obedience and concern for people.

The quality of Philip's life resulted in his being given a commission, along with six other deacons to care for the church widows (Acts 6). This was God's proving ground. Having shown himself faithful in this area he was soon moved on to areas of greater significance and impact.

The persecution of Christians in Jerusalem resulted in his taking up an evangelistic ministry in the main city of Samaria. Clearly this was the Spirit's strategy for introducing the gospel to a different culture, and of course we have a lesson here on the sovereign over-ruling purposes of God.

Probably Philip's greatest test was the call to leave the known, the fruitful and the exciting circumstances of Samaria for the unknown situation awaiting him on the Jerusalem-Gaza road. 'And he arose and went.' What a wealth of meaning is in these words!

In his talk with the Ethiopian treasurer he proves himself an able personal worker and has the joy of leading him to Christ.

We don't know just how Philip was 'spirited away' from this scene, but the Scripture does record that he makes every part of his journey count as he works his way northwards from Azotus (the Philistine Ashdod) to the port of Caesarea.

A final note in Acts 21 indicates that he must have married and made his home in Caesarea; his four daughters all became keen Christians with the gift of prophecy.

How do we understand the word 'prophetess'? Some say that prophecy is a spiritual gift whereby, without volition or rationalization, a person is enabled by the direct action of the Holy Spirit to speak a message from God. Others feel that such a gift is not relevant or needed today. Still others feel that to be a prophet means holding forth the teachings of the Scripture with such authority and relevance that the hearers recognize the authentic mark of the Spirit in what the speaker has chosen to say.

Paul certainly upheld the value and significance of this gift (1 Cor. 14:1-11) which was exercised by both men and women (1 Cor. 11:4, 5).

STUDY 11

STEPHEN – THE FIRST OF A NOBLE LINE

QUESTIONS

DAY 1 *Acts 6:1-5.*

a) Stephen is described as being 'full of faith'. What does it mean to be 'full of faith' in practical terms?

b) Why should the candidates have to be 'full of the Holy Spirit' for such a mundane job?

DAY 2 *Acts 6:3-8.*

a) Were the 'twelve' self-centred in refusing to get involved in this bit of practical Christianity?

b) In verse 8 Stephen is again described as being 'full of faith' – but also of 'power'. What exactly is 'power'? What would the evidence of 'power' in your life be?

DAY 3 *Acts 6:9-15.*

a) What is the evidence that Stephen was indeed full of the Holy Spirit (vv. 3 and 5) and had the gift of wisdom?

b) Is it possible for a facial expression to have a spiritual source? (Do you ever pray about the impact of your gestures, tone of voice, facial expression, limb movements? This is called 'body language' and it communicates, even when we are unconscious of it.)

DAY 4 *Acts 7:20-42.*

a) Why do you think Stephen made so much of the experience of Moses in his address to the synagogue? (See especially vv. 27, 35, 39, 52.)

b) What solemn warning can you see in the phrase, 'God gave them up' in verse 42? (See also Rom. 1:24, 26, 28.)

DAY 5 *Acts 7:51-54.*

a) Verse 51 indicates that it is possible to resist the Holy Spirit. It also seems possible to grieve Him (Eph. 4:30), quench or smother Him (1 Thess. 5:19), lie to Him (Acts 5:3), and insult Him (Heb. 10:29). What is the lesson of these verses for you?

b) What does it mean to be 'stiff-necked and uncircumcised in head and ears'? What are the perils of spiritual insensitivity?

DAY 6 *Acts 7:54-60.*

a) What was the final affront that triggered Stephen's murderers?

b) What was the moment of supreme victory for Stephen? (How do you react when criticized?)

DAY 7 *Acts 8:1-8.*

a) 'The blood of the martyrs is the seed of the church.' What illustration of that truth do we have here?

b) Review the whole story. What benefits for the individual Christian come through opposition or persecution?

NOTES

Stephen's name comes from the Greek 'Stephanos' which means 'CROWN', and he was surely well-named. He was Christianity's first martyr, the first recipient of the martyr's crown.

His story begins in Acts 6 when he was chosen with six others to care for the Christian widows. The wording of the passage clearly indicates that in terms of spiritual intensity and faith he was the most outstanding. It is obvious that along with the practical 'social welfare' task he also exercised a telling and powerful public ministry accompanied by miraculous events.

Synagogues were open for visiting speakers to give their message. It was in one of these that Greek-speaking Jews were so vehement in their opposition to the message of salvation that they actually paid witnesses to give false evidence before the Sanhedrin (the highest Jewish court) about Stephen's teaching.

Stephen's defence is worthy of careful study and some of the questions set will ask you to spot the main line he takes, a fearless line that shows up his accusers for what they really are. (See especially 7:51.)

His final remarks about 'seeing Jesus standing at the right hand of God' were too much for his accusers. They grabbed him, took him outside the city and stoned him to death.

It is a sobering thought that the persecution of Christians in our generation has been just as great, if not greater, than at any time in history. Are we taking our freedom too lightly? Do we take our open Bible and our open churches for granted?

Notice it was Stephen's testimony to seeing Jesus that finally 'brought the house down'. Watch this in your witnessing. People don't get too upset as long as you talk vaguely about God, but start telling them of the Lord Jesus and the change He makes in a man's life and you will see the opposition's true colour.

Why such opposition? Why persecution? Why don't people just ignore us, if we're so crazy? The truth is that the Enemy doesn't leave vital witnessing Christians alone! He is behind all persecution and martyrdom. Beware of things going too easy for you!

ANSWER GUIDE

The following pages contain an Answer Guide. It is recommended that answers to the questions be attempted before turning to this guide. It is only a guide and the answers given should not be treated as exhaustive.

GUIDE TO STUDY 1

DAY 1

a) Righteous before God; walking in all the commandments of God; blameless.
b) Sarah, Rebekah, Rachel, Samson's mother, Hannah.
c) Sharing within the group.

DAY 2

a) Perseverance in prayer.
b) Personal.

DAY 3

a) Great; teetotaller; Spirit filled. He would turn many Israelites to God and would be the prophet who would prepare the people for the coming of Christ.
b) By example in godly living; by loving discipline; by praying for and with our children and teaching them the Bible; by always being available to listen to and advise them.

DAY 4

a) Children were considered a sign of God's blessing to a couple.
b) There are many doors open to women today, but true fulfilment is found in serving God and others, whether through motherhood or otherwise.

DAY 5

a) By the inspiration of the Holy Spirit.
b) That Mary's baby would be her Lord, the Son of God.
c) They would talk about the prophecies of the Bible, and how blessed they both were in being part of their fulfilment. They would discuss how they should bring up their children in the ways of God. They would probably pray about Joseph's attitude towards the news of Mary's pregnancy on her return. They would spend much time in fellowship and prayer together.

DAY 6

a) They rejoiced with her.
b) To accept them as a loan from God and to bring them up to know Him.
c) The fruit of love, joy, peace, patience, kindness, goodness, faithfulness, gentleness and self-control. Also the fruit of bringing people to Jesus and encouraging believers.

DAY 7

a) They were both described in the same terms as godly people; they were supportive of each other, Elizabeth accepting all Zechariah told her; they were of one mind in naming the child.
b) Her husband received back his ability to speak, and began to praise and glorify God.

c) That the example and teaching that children receive from their parents during their earliest years are vitally important and remain with them through life.

GUIDE TO STUDY 2

DAY 1

a) She was not married but had not grasped the fact that the virgin of Isaiah 7:14 was to have a Son without a human father.
b) God does not force His will on us. He shows us His will but requires our co-operation to bring it about.

DAY 2

a) She would probably have to struggle with fear, but would have the assurance that God would vindicate her.
b) The miracle God had done for Elizabeth would strengthen her faith.
It would assure her that godly men would recognize who her Son was.
She would further be assured that this Son was to be the Saviour of the whole world.

DAY 3

a) God revealed His plans to both partners. Joseph cared for Mary and she trusted his leadership. They loved each other, and together cared for the Son. We can learn to experience harmony in marriage relationships and in parenthood.
b) Widowhood would draw them closer as they together cared for the younger members of the family.

DAY 4

a) 'Woman' was a term of respect. Note, Jesus used it in His concern for Mary while on the cross. He was gently showing her that He could no longer take orders from her, but only from God. He would do only what God showed Him to do.
b) Verse 5.
c) Total obedience to Him would bring true fulfilment to our lives.

DAY 5

a) They no doubt wanted to persuade him to soft-pedal as opposition increased. His close relationships from then on had to be with those who believed in Him, even more than with His natural family.
b) Where family desires conflict with God's will, obedience to God must come first. Though we should seek to please our family we may feel a greater affinity with our spiritual family.

DAY 6

a) Mary suffered greatly as she saw the growing opposition to her Son which culminated in His arrest, trial and crucifixion.
b) Her love for her Son took her as far as the cross. She had the consolation of knowing that her love and presence would be a comfort to Him. His thinking of her and committing her to the care of John must have been a great comfort.

c) Most of the apostles and many others, e.g. Peter was beaten and imprisoned, yet wrote I Peter I:8. Paul suffered much, yet continually wrote about joy.

DAY 7 a) Acceptance, knowing that He is with us in it.
b) She sees her family becoming disciples of Jesus.
c) Perhaps: 'Now that I have seen the glorious outcome of the death and resurrection of my Son in opening up salvation for the world, any sacrifice I made has been well rewarded.'

GUIDE TO STUDY 3

DAY 1 a) A woman who receives definite messages from God to give to His people.
b) Miriam; Deborah; Huldah.

DAY 2 By reminding ourselves that we will be reunited with those who have died with their faith in Jesus. By looking to the Lord, His word and His people for comfort and encouragement. By getting involved in serving other people, and so finding an outlet for the desire to love and be loved.

DAY 3 a) It is possible only by cultivating an attitude of 'practising His presence,' quick repentance and of praising God in all circumstances. Every matter we read or hear about can be turned into prayer.
b) Moses; Elijah; Hannah; David; Daniel; Jesus; Paul, etc.
c) The prayers of the Pharisees were insincere, with the desire to draw attention to themselves, and effected no change in their lives. These other men and women of prayer prayed with real burden, with repentance and with faith, usually apart from public gaze. Their prayers were combined with praise and worship.

DAY 4 a) Yes.
b) It is usually at times of crisis or when important decisions have to be made, especially where there is a burden for a certain person, church, district or nation, that prayer and fasting is practised. Fasting shows sincerity of purpose.

DAY 5 a) A picture of the bodies of believers in which the Holy Spirit resides to enable us to worship and serve God.
b) We can be guilty of defiling it by any of the sins of the flesh: immorality, gluttony, overindulgence in alcohol, drugs, tobacco, etc. By laziness, uncleanness, insufficient rest, or anything that renders our bodies less fit for His use.

DAY 6 a) Because, although we have not seen the Saviour, we know that we have been redeemed by His sacrifice on the cross.
b) Praise turns our attention on God who is bigger than all our problems. It produces faith, joy, peace and victory.

c) Jesus in facing the cross; David when faced by his enemies; Jonah while in the fish's belly; Paul and Silas in prison.

DAY 7

a) That of being His witness to everyone she met.
b) Mary Magdalene.
c) Because Jesus commands it and gives the Holy Spirit to empower us; because Jesus is no longer here, but has appointed us as His ambassadors; because without the knowledge of Jesus, people will die in their sins. He died for all, and all have a right to know.

GUIDE TO STUDY 4

DAY 1

a) Mary met Jesus' emotional need for fellowship and Martha His practical need for food.
b) Mary's emotional temperament can lead to thoughtlessness toward the more practical person. Martha's practical temperament could lead to a judgmental attitude towards the less practical person.
c) She was getting worried and distracted and also resentful towards Mary. When the 'cares of this life' rob us of our peace, we can show the same faults.

DAY 2

a) Their mutual concern for their brother in his illness.
b) He loved each one.
c) We can know that, in spite of our faults, He still loves us.

DAY 3

a) To strengthen their faith. It seems Lazarus would have been dead even if Jesus had gone at once (he had been dead four days – v. 39); but the miracle of resurrection would have been greater after decomposition had set in.
b) Jesus was thinking of others, the disciples of their personal safety.
c) Example: So long as Jesus, the Light of the world, is with us, we can face life triumphantly; without Him we will stumble.

DAY 4

a) She had faith that Jesus had power to heal and that God would grant whatever He asked.
b) By believing that all blessings will be ours in heaven rather than experiencing Christ's victory now.
c) That He is the one who raises the dead. We can know that if we, as believers die, He will raise us to life. If we are still alive at His return, we shall never die.
d) Peter.

DAY 5

a) By telling her that Jesus wanted to see her.
b) They had been saying to each other that if only Jesus had been there, their brother wouldn't have died. Both had faith in His power to heal.

DAY 6 a) In her brother being raised to life after being dead four days.
b) Compassion for the two sisters; to reveal His power; to assure us of our own resurrection.

DAY 7 a) We can serve others. Jesus accepts such service as done to Himself.
b) It is a ministry for all, but let us not make Martha's mistake of putting more emphasis on the food than on the fellowship (Matt. 10:42).

GUIDE TO STUDY 5

DAY 1 a) The epileptic boy, the girl with a spirit of divination.
b) Jesus.
c) To believers in Him.

DAY 2 a) By supplying His material needs, and giving Him love and companionship.
b) Yes, by caring for His children in need, and by witnessing about Jesus to enable the Gospel to reach others.

DAY 3 a) Jesus' mother.
b) Yes. The church gathered to pray while Peter was in prison awaiting execution, etc.
c) They put Jesus' needs before their own fears and grief. They showed great love, selflessness and courage in the face of danger.

DAY 4 a) To pour sweet spices on His body, according to custom.
b) There was a great stone blocking the entrance.
c) That Christian women can work together as a team for Jesus.

DAY 5 a) On several occasions He had told them He would rise from the dead. (Matt. 16:21; 17:9; 20:19, etc.)
b) To show that Jesus had already been raised and had left the tomb.
c) The women believed though they were still perplexed, whereas the apostles refused to believe.

DAY 6 a) She was probably still struggling with doubt and desperately wanted to see Him.
b) My Lord. Personal.
c) Verse 15.

DAY 7 a) She was probably not facing Him and was blinded by tears.
b) She recognized His voice as He spoke her name. (The gardener would hardly have known it.)
c) Personal.
d) By witnessing to the disciples that she had actually seen Him alive from the dead. By telling everyone about her personal encounter with her risen Lord. By doing as Mary did.

GUIDE TO STUDY 6

DAY 1

a) Their true spirituality was evidenced by: bold witnessing (v. 33); unity (v. 32); surrender of material possessions for the use of the fellowship (v. 32).
b) Personal answer. Note that the teaching in James 2 indicates that a true walk with the Lord has very practical outworkings.

DAY 2

a) His sympathetic concern and positive outlook. (You will see the same in his Antioch experience in tomorrow's reacting.)
b) The churches had a surge of spiritual and numerical growth. Paul's own witness and ministry now contributed to this.

DAY 3

a) His good testimony. He had proved himself in the handling of Paul and this was a similar situation.
b) Barnabas had noted Paul's capability for ministry after his conversion and saw his potential for helping these new converts.

DAY 4

a) Probably both approaches should be held together in balance. The individual certainly needs to be sure of God's leading but the fellowship should be bold and sufficiently concerned for others to encourage their best young people to think of cross-cultural ministry.
'One man gives freely, yet gains even more; another withholds unduly, but comes to poverty' (Prov. 11:24).
b) Fasting. The true objective of fasting is to liberate us from human and worldly influences and rational thinking so that we can discern the mind of the Lord and have faith strengthened.
c) It was the home territory of Barnabas and so provided a natural starting point for their tour.

DAY 5

a) At first they were treated as gods, latterly as enemies.
b) This episode warns us of the fickleness of popularity. Be God-pleasers not men-pleasers! (Eph. 6:6).
c) A concern for the new Christians (v. 22). Timothy was the reward! From the place of greatest persecution God gave Paul his best co-worker! (Phil. 2:20).

DAY 6

a) They were men who risked their lives for the gospel and were proven in their love and concern for the growth of new Christians. Their testimony would add to the impact of the message (v. 26).
b) That Christians should be capable of discerning the mind of the Lord and that the Holy Spirit's peace in each heart is the confirmation of this (Col. 3:15).

DAY 7

a) Mark had left them suddenly. Barnabas was proved right because Paul evidently changed his mind and later described Mark as a 'useful worker'.
b) Disagreements tend to become dislikes in the heart of a stubborn person. True spirituality requires continuing commitment to each other as fellow Christians, even though differences of opinion do occur.
c) Discussion on personal findings.

GUIDE TO STUDY 7

DAY 1

a) Possibly because he knew that she would organize prayer for him.
b) He would be impressed at such a speedy answer to prayer.
c) Yes! Prayer groups in the home are likely to be – more informal and relaxed than in a church building; preceded by relevant sharing by participants; attended by those who 'mean business'.

DAY 2

a) The objectives were two-fold: experience and maturity.
b) A group of mature concerned Christians meeting for worship and prayer were sensitive to the Holy Spirit's leading.
c) Individuals do need a sense of calling but the fellowship is equally responsible for encouraging them to launch out and for supporting them when they go. See Philippians 4:10-15 for a precedent.

DAY 3

a) We don't know exactly why Mark left them but obviously Paul felt he did not have a strong enough reason, but the less severe and more positive Barnabas saw Mark's potential and decided to encourage him.
b) Barnabas was proved to be right because Mark made good in the end, having overcome whatever weakness that had previously existed.
Personal answer. The big lesson is 'failure need never be final'.

DAY 4

a) Mark went on to be a very effective Christian worker.
b) He had a gift of writing in which graphic detail and fast action are the main features.

DAY 5

a) How to present the meaning of the death and resurrection of Jesus (v. 30-32). How to be joyful and victorious in spite of difficulty and opposition (v. 52). How to expose the state of heart of those who rejected the message of the gospel (v. 41).
b) His unique conversion, his education and training helped equip Paul for ministry to the Gentile world.

DAY 6

a) Faith is the key which releases the power of God (vv. 23, 24).
b) The exorcism of stubborn demons demands perseverance in faith and prayer until they yield to Christ's authority (v. 29).

DAY 7

a) Mark.
b) Mark's.
c) Mark's.
d) Personal answer. Probably the marvellous 'turn around' made by Mark after his failure and his subsequent usefulness in the work of the gospel.

GUIDE TO STUDY 8

DAY 1

a) A disciple is a Christian who has accepted the principle of the cross (Luke 14:27; Gal. 2:20), has a quality of relationship with the Saviour that

makes him a blessing to others (John 15:5-8), is concerned about walking in the light and love with his fellow Christians (John 13:35, I John 1:7), and is a purposeful student of the Word, intent upon applying spiritual truths to his life and thereby growing towards maturity (John 8:31, 32).
b) Because a true disciple is someone who is seeking an intimate relationship with Himself, and will thus be a reproducer of other disciples.

DAY 2

a) His good testimony before other Christians (16:2); his good family training; his potential as a future Christian worker.
b) He was stoned, beaten up and left for dead.
c) God gave Paul his most valuable co-worker out of the town which gave him the roughest treatment.

DAY 3

a) The lesson of sensitivity – walking closely with God and finding out His will (16:10); the blessing of responsiveness to guidance given – being led to Lydia so that her spiritual need could be met (16:13, 14); fellowship in decision-making, observing the unity with which the team moved (16:10); observing Paul's handling of opposition squarely and authoritatively in the Name of Jesus (16:18); principles of church growth (16:5).
b) Because God wanted him to have a wider and deeper vision and to take the gospel to the continent of Europe. Others could follow the familiar Phyrgia-Galatia trail but it needed a man of Paul's qualities to pioneer in a new culture.

DAY 4

a) Timothy had a selfless attitude towards the needs of others and gave himself consistently in caring for their spiritual needs.
b) He wanted to know how they were faring because he was deeply concerned about their spiritual growth.
c) Paul had confidence in Timothy and trusted him.

DAY 5

a) We get the picture of someone who probably had a low self-image and didn't stand up for himself too well (I Cor. 16:10, 11; I Tim. 4:12). He was possibly rather timid (2 Timothy 1:4); did not seem to enjoy robust health (I Tim. 5:23).
b) The lesson for us is that God is not looking for a lot of human talent and aggressiveness, but for those who, in spite of the consciousness of their limitations, make themselves available for the Lord's service.
c) Personal answer (see the following passages which list spiritual gifts: Rom. 12; I Cor. 12 – 2 lists; Eph. 4; I Pet. 4:10, 11).

DAY 6

a) His mother and grandmother were zealous Christians and had given him a good upbringing and had trained him in the Old Testament Scriptures.
b) With the parents (Prov. 13:1; 22:6).

DAY 7

a) The pattern is for every disciple to invest his knowledge of the Lord in another person, ensuring that they grasp the truth so effectively that they can in turn invest in others.

b) Obedience (2 Tim. 2:4); Discipline (v. 4); Dedication (v. 4); Sacrifice (v. 3); Ability to weather spiritual conflict (2 Tim. 2:3; I Tim. I:18).

GUIDE TO STUDY 9

DAY I

a) Yes! Any form of identification with others is a legitimate bridge for the gospel. Jesus used his need of water to get through to the woman of Sychar (John 4).
b) Don't back off before they fully understand the implications of your message. Paul was preaching in a synagogue and his audience would have a knowledge of the Old Testament scriptures. Every situation needs to be evaluated on its own merit.

DAY 2

a) A personal answer.
b) They saw it as a means to an end rather than as an end in itself.

DAY 3

a) The literal rendering of Romans I6:5 is, 'greet their in-house church'. So it was obviously used for church activities, worship, fellowship and teaching.
b) They were completely 'sold out' to the work of God's Kingdom, holding nothing back, in contrast to Ananias and Sapphira who made out they had surrendered everything but hadn't.

DAY 4

a) They were a team in the work of the Lord.
b) For prayer meetings (Acts I2:I2); for evangelism (Acts I6:32; II:I2-I5); for hospitality (Acts I6:I5); for teaching new converts (Acts I8:II); for fellowship (Col. 4:I5; Philem. 2).
Risk, sacrifice and commitment to the Lordship of Christ regardless of cost.

DAY 5

Personal answer. C. T. Studd's (the Founder of WEC) motto was, 'If Jesus Christ be God and died for me then no sacrifice can be too great for me to make for Him.'

DAY 6

a) He was a conscientious Christian worker who was deeply concerned for the spiritual development of the Colossian Christians.
b) Personal answer.

DAY 7

a) His consuming desire was that the Colossian Christians should come to maturity, and be absolutely confident about God's purpose for their lives (Col. 4:I2).
b) Personal answer.
Intercession implies accepting full responsibility for another in need, and not 'letting go' until the need is met.

GUIDE TO STUDY 10

DAY 1

a) They were justified in not becoming involved because they already had a set of God-given goals (see v. 4).
b) Personal answer. The dangers are that we tend, unconsciously, to feel that they are inferior in ability, and so adopt a 'paternal' condescending attitude which is quickly detected.

DAY 2

a) They were to be men who had a good testimony, were filled with the Spirit and were wise in judgment.
b) To be 'filled with the Spirit' means being sensitive to the Holy Spirit's leading, bringing one's life under the Lordship of Christ and adopting a discipleship lifestyle that is in keeping with the teaching of the Scriptures. (See Luke 14:27; Gal. 5:22-24; 2 Tim. 1:7.)

DAY 3

a) Men meant it for evil but God allowed it and used the scattering of the Christians to spread the Gospel. It would seem that Christians in countries where there is a repressive regime are much stronger and deeper in their faith and more aggressive in their witness than Christians in the West. See Romans 5:3-5 for the sequence of God's purpose in letting Christians be under pressure.
b) He was spontaneous in his witnessing, and obviously knew the power of God in exorcising demons and praying for the sick.
c) Personal.

DAY 4

a) It must have been hard to leave a fruitful sphere of evangelistic endeavour and move to an unknown desert situation with no clear knowledge of what he was to do. He was successful and fruitful because he did exactly what the Lord told him to do.
b) Someone to explain the Scriptures and lead him to Christ.

DAY 5

a) Yes. When God burdens us for someone's spiritual need, we can trust Him to prepare his/her heart to receive the word.
b) He was able to **apply** the portion to the **need** of the Ethiopian. This implies both understanding and perception.
c) Yes. The issue of faith in Christ requires a decision, and because he sensed the man's heart had been prepared by the Holy Spirit (otherwise why should he have bought the scroll in Jerusalem and be trying to read it in a joggling chariot on a dirt road?).

DAY 6

a) The good personal worker will always stress the need for making up one's mind about salvation, but he will also be sensitive to the degree of preparation and readiness which exists in the inquirer's heart.
b) Personal answer. God means us to be world Christians! (Not world-ly Christians!) Indeed by inference from Matthew 28:18-20 a disciple is a person

who is prepared to be involved in disciple-making across cultural barriers, either by direct action, prayer, support or the motivation and teaching of others on this concept. (Note:'nations' = 'ethnic groups,' Greek, ethne.)

DAY 7

His four daughters were believers and had the gift of prophecy. A Christian worker underlines and reinforces the quality of his service by having an exemplary family life. (Note that a basic qualification for church eldership is that his family is orderly, co-operative and well-behaved, I Tim. 3:4, 5.)
The influence of parents both by precept and example is incalculable. Many Christian workers testify to the foundation of their faith in their family upbringing.

GUIDE TO STUDY 11

DAY 1

a) Possible answers: Stephen looked at life through the eyes of faith, i.e. he saw every situation as under God's sovereignty; he was capable of trusting the Lord in negative circumstances; he had such a high degree of positive trust in God that his life was a challenge and blessing to those who met him.
b) Being full of the Holy Spirit really means being fully under the control of the Holy Spirit; every Christian servant, no matter how 'unimportant' his task, can do it under the Spirit's control, and so bring glory to God and blessing to others.

DAY 2

a) No. They had their God-given priorities (Do you? If so you can say 'no' to good, but low-priority, activities.)
b) Power is the ability to accomplish what we are designed to do. The engine of a bus has power to pull a load of sixty people. A spider has power to weave a gossamer thread. 2 Timothy 1:7 says God has not given us the spirit of fear, but the spirit of power (dunamis = ability to accomplish – 'can do') love and self-control. The evidence of power in one's life is the successful accomplishment of the tasks that are God's will for us.

DAY 3

a) The Jews were confounded by Stephen's wisdom and forceful arguments.
b) Yes. This remark has been made about many facing martyrdom. It was said of Bill McChesney, a WEC missionary in Congo, just before he was killed by the Simba rebels in 1964.

DAY 4

a) Because episodes of Moses' life depicted by Stephen have a common theme – rejection. This was exactly what his hearers were doing with the message of salvation through Christ.
b) Beyond a certain point God will stop in His efforts to convince people of the errors of their ways. 'My Spirit will not always strive with man' (Gen. 6:3).

DAY 5 a) One lesson is that the Holy Spirit really is a person, a sensitive person. Although other passages stress His power we have also to recognize that He can be resisted and rejected.
b) It means to block out the message of God's Spirit in our hearts. The degree of insensitivity increases as it is allowed to continue; people can become harder and harder in rejecting the Word of the Lord.

DAY 6 a) The crunch was the assertion that he could actually see Jesus, the One whom they were determined to reject.
b) Stephen's supreme moment was when he prayed for forgiveness for those who were murdering him (v. 60). Note our Lord's experience in Luke 23:34.

DAY 7 a) Paul must have been profoundly moved by Stephen's experience. It is significant that he had a similar revelation of Christ at the moment of his conversion.
b) Faith is strengthened, love is deepened, the true nature of the world's opposition is seen, and a deeper awareness of the indwelling presence of Christ is created. Note the connection between suffering and glory in I Peter 4.

OLD TESTAMENT

The Beginning of Everything: A Study in Genesis 1-11 ISBN 978-0-90806-728-2
Triumphs Over Failures: A Study in Judges ISBN 978-1-85792-888-4
The Throne and Temple: A Study in 1 & 2 Chronicles ISBN 978-185792-910-2
Faith, Courage and Perserverance: A Study in Ezra ISBN 978-185792-949-2
Comfort and Encouragement: A Study in Psalms 1 - 50 ISBN 978-1-84550-408-3
A Saviour is Promised: A Study in Isaiah 1 - 39 ISBN 978-090806-755-8
Our Magnificent God: A Study in Isaiah 40 - 66 ISBN 978-185792-909-6
The Cost of Obedience: A Study in Jeremiah ISBN 978-0-90806-761-9
Hypocrisy in Religion: A Study in Amos ISBN 978-090806-706-0
Amazing Love: A Study in Hosea ISBN 978-1-84550-004-0
Unshakeable Confidence: A Study in Habakkuk & Joel ISBN 978-090806-751-0
Messenger of Love: A Study in Malachi ISBN 978-1-85792-885-3
Focus on Faith: A Study of 10 Old Testament Characters ISBN 978-185792-890-7

NEW TESTAMENT

Glimpses of the King: A Study in Matthew's Gospel ISBN 978-1-84550-007-8
A Message for Today: A Study in Mark's Gospel ISBN 978-1-84550-413-7
The World's Only Hope: A Study in Luke's Gospel ISBN 978-185792-886-0
Jesus, Who is He? A Study in John's Gospel ISBN 978-090806-716-9
The Early Church: A Study in Acts 1-12 ISBN 978-090806-736-7
Wordwide Evangelisation: A Study in Acts 13-28 ISBN 978-1-84550-005-4
The Only Way to be Good: A Study in Romans ISBN 978-185792-950-8
People and Problems in the Church: A Study in 1 Corinthians ISBN 978-1-84550-021-4
Controlled by Love: A Study in 2 Corinthians ISBN 978-1-84550-022-1
Born to be Free: A Study in Galatians ISBN 978-1-84550-019-1
Heavenly Living: A Study in Ephesians ISBN 978-185792-911-9
Made Completely New: A Study in Colossians & Philemon ISBN 978-0-90806-721-3
Get Ready: A Study in 1&2 Thessalonians ISBN 978-185792-948-5
Entering by Faith: A Study in Hebrews ISBN 978-185792-914-0
Faith that Works: A Study in James ISBN 978-090806-701-5
Walking in Love: A Study in John's Epistles ISBN 978-185792-891-4
Drama of Revelation: A Study in Revelation ISBN 978-1-84550-020-2

CHARACTERS

Abraham: A Study of Genesis 12-25 ISBN 978-185792-887-7
The Man God Chose: A Study in the Life of Jacob ISBN 978-1-84550-025-2
God plans for Good: A Study of Joseph ISBN 978-090806-700-8
Meek but Mighty: A Study of Moses ISBN 978-1-85792-951-5
Serving the Lord: A Study of Joshua ISBN 978-185792-889-1
A Man After God's Own Heart: A Study of David ISBN 978-090806-746-6
A Man with a Choice: A Study in the Life of Solomon ISBN 978-1-84550-023-8
Men of Courage: A Study of Elijah & Elisha ISBN 978-185792-913-3
Grace & Grit: A Study of Ruth & Esther ISBN 978-185792-909-9
Highly Esteemed: A Study in the Life of Daniel ISBN 978-1-84550-006-1
God Cares: A Study in the Life of Jonah ISBN 978-1-84550-024-5
Achieving the Impossible: A Study of Nehemiah ISBN 978-090806-707-7

THEMES

God's Heart, My Heart: World Mission ISBN 978-185792-892-1
Freedom: You Can Find it! ISBN 978-090806-702-2
Freely Forgiven: A Study in Redemption ISBN 978-090806-720-6
The Problems of Life! Is there an Answer? ISBN 978-185792-907-2
Understanding the Way of Salvation ISBN 978-090082-880-5
Saints in Service: 12 Bible Characters ISBN 978-185792-912-6
Finding Christ in the Old Testament: Pre-existence and Prophecy ISBN 978-0-90806-739-8
Finding Life's Purpose: A Study in Discipleship ISBN 978-1-84550-409-0
Discovering God's Glory: What God is Really Like ISBN 978-1-84550-410-6
Future and Hope: What the Bible is All About ISBN 978-1-84550-411-3
Love and Respect: A Biblical View of Godly Relationships ISBN 978-1-84550-412-0

GEARED FOR GROWTH BIBLE STUDIES

Enable you to:

1. Have a daily encounter with God
2. Encourage you to apply the Word of God to everyday life
3. Help you to share your faith with others
4. They are straightforward, practical, non-controversial and inexpensive.

WEC INTERNATIONAL is involved in gospel outreach, church planting and discipleship training using every possible means including radio, literature, medical work, rural development schemes, correspondence courses and telephone counselling. Nearly two thousand workers are involved in their fields and sending bases.

Find out more from the following Website:
www.wec-int.org.uk

A full list of over 50 'Geared for Growth' studies can be obtained from:

UK GEARED FOR GROWTH COORDINATORS

John and Ann Edwards
8, Sidings Terrace, Skewen, Neath, W.Glam, SA10 6RE
Email: rhysjohn.edwards@virgin.net
Tel. 01792 814994

UK Website: www.gearedforgrowth.co.uk

For information on Geared for Growth Bible Studies in other languages contact:

Word Worldwide International Coordinators
Kip and Doreen Wear
Tel. 01269 870842
Email: kip.wear@virgin.net

Christian Focus Publications
Publishes books for all ages

Our mission statement –
STAYING FAITHFUL
In dependence upon God we seek to help make His infallible word, the Bible, relevant. Our aim is to ensure that the Lord Jesus Christ is presented as the only hope to obtain forgiveness of sin, live a useful life and look forward to heaven with Him.
REACHING OUT
Christ's last command requires us to reach out to our world with His gospel. We seek to help fulfil that by publishing books that point people towards Jesus and help them to develop a Christ-like maturity. We aim to equip all levels of readers for life, work, ministry and mission.

Books in our adult range are published in three imprints.
Christian Focus contains popular works including biographies, commentaries, basic doctrine, and Christian living. Our children's books are published in this imprint.
Mentor focuses on books written at a level suitable for Bible College and seminary students, pastors, and other serious readers. The imprint includes commentaries, doctrinal studies, examination of current issues, and church history.
Christian Heritage contains classic writings from the past.

For details of our titles visit us on our website
www.christianfocus.com

ISBN 978-1-85792-912-6

Published in 2008 by
Christian Focus Publications, Geanies House,
Fearn, Ross-shire, IV20 1TW, Scotland
and
WEC International, Bulstrode, Oxford Road,
Gerrards Cross, Bucks, SL9 8SZ

Cover design by Alister MacInnes

Printed and bound by Bell & Bain Ltd., Glasgow